Ready to Read
Consonant Blends and More Vowels

How to Play

1. Press the Power button to turn the SD-X Reader on or off. The LED will light up when the SD-X Reader is on.

2. Touch the volume buttons found on this page to adjust the volume.

3. Touch words and pictures on the page to hear audio. The monkey gives instructions and starts activities.

4. After two minutes of inactivity, the SD-X Reader will beep and go to sleep.

5. If the batteries are low, the SD-X Reader will beep twice and the LED will start blinking. Replace the batteries by following the instructions on the next page. The SD-X Reader uses two AAA batteries.

6. To use headphones or earbuds, plug them into the headphone jack on the SD-X Reader.

Volume

 Publications International, Ltd.

Battery Information

Includes two replaceable AAA batteries (UM-4 or LR03).

Battery Installation

1. Open battery door with small flat-head or Phillips screwdriver.
2. Install new batteries according to +/- polarity. If batteries are not installed properly, the device will not function.
3. Replace battery door; secure with small screw.

Battery Safety

Batteries must be replaced by adults only. Properly dispose of used batteries. See battery manufacturer for disposal recommendations. Do not mix alkaline, standard (carbon-zinc), or rechargeable (nickel-cadmium) batteries. Do not mix old and new batteries. Only recommended batteries of the same or equivalent type should be used. Remove weakened or dead batteries. Never short-circuit the supply terminals. Non-rechargeable batteries are not to be recharged. Do not use rechargeable batteries. If batteries are swallowed, in the USA, promptly see a doctor and have the doctor phone 1-202-625-3333 collect. In other countries, have the doctor call your local poison control center. This product uses 2 AAA batteries (2 X 1.5V = 3.0 V). Use batteries of the same or equivalent type as recommended. The supply terminals are not to be short-circuited. Batteries should be changed when sounds mix, distort, or become otherwise unintelligible as batteries weaken. The electrostatic discharge may interfere with the sound module. If this occurs, please simply restart the sound module by pressing any key.

In Europe, the dustbin symbol indicates that batteries, rechargeable batteries, button cells, battery packs, and similar materials must not be discarded in household waste. Batteries containing hazardous substances are harmful to the environment and to health. Please help to protect the environment from health risks by telling your children to dispose of batteries properly and by taking batteries to local collection points. Batteries handled in this manner are safely recycled.

Warning: Changes or modifications to this unit not expressly approved by the party responsible for compliance could void the user's authority to operate the equipment.

NOTE: This equipment has been tested and found to comply with the limits for a Class B digital device, pursuant to Part 15 of the FCC Rules. These limits are designed to provide reasonable protection against harmful interference in a residential installation. This equipment generates, uses, and can radiate radio frequency energy and, if not installed and used in accordance with the instructions, may cause harmful interference to radio communications. However, there is no guarantee that interference will not occur in a particular installation. If this equipment does cause harmful interference to radio or television reception, which can be determined by turning the equipment off and on, the user is encouraged to try to correct the interference by one or more of the following measures: Reorient or relocate the receiving antenna. Increase the separation between the equipment and receiver. Connect the equipment into an outlet on a circuit different from that to which the receiver is connected. Consult the dealer or an experienced radio TV technician for help.

Contributing Writers: Natalie Goldstein, Anne Schreiber, Lisa Trumbauer, Michele Warrence-Schreiber

Consultants: Susan A. Miller, Ed.D., Dr. Leslie Anne Perry

Illustrators: James Schlottman, George Ulrich

Picture Credits: Comstock RF; Corbis RF; Image Club Graphics; PhotoDisc; PIL Collection; StockByte

Copyright © 2011 Publications International, Ltd.

Product and sound element design, engineering, and reproduction are proprietary technologies of Publications International, Ltd.

Louis Weber, C.E.O., Publications International, Ltd.

7373 North Cicero Avenue   Ground Floor, 59 Gloucester Place
Lincolnwood, Illinois 60712   London W1U 8JJ

Customer Service:

1-888-724-0144 or customer_service@pilbooks.com
www.pilbooks.com

SD-X Interactive is a registered trademark in the United States and Canada.

Manufactured in China.

8 7 6 5 4 3 2 1
ISBN-10: 1-4508-2064-6
ISBN-13: 978-1-4508-2064-6

Shhh. Check It Out!

Sh and **ch** are consonant blends that make similar sounds.

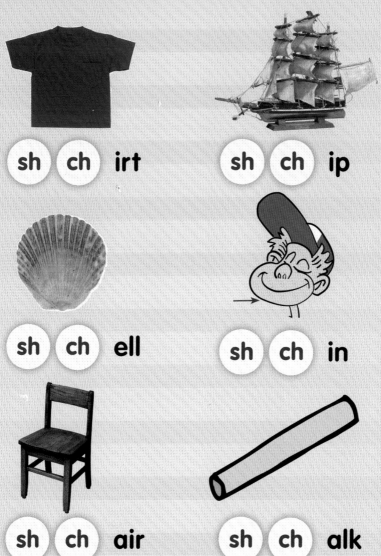

sh ch irt

sh ch ip

sh ch ell

sh ch in

sh ch air

sh ch alk

Love Those Shoes!

Recognize **th** sound.

When **t** and **h** are combined in a word, they make the **th** sound.

Do you like these shoes?

I bought them today!

They fit better than my old shoes.

I tried on that pair of shoes, too.

Then I tried on this pair.

They are the best shoes ever!

Thanks a Lot!

Recognize **th** sound.

theater	thirteen	thirty
thumb	thimble	thread

30

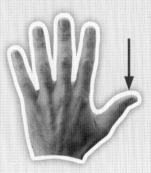

13

Let's Blend

Identify **cr**, **dr**, and **br** blends.

The letter **r** can be added to other letters to make new consonant blends.

Greasy Fries

Grandpa Frank and Grandma Fran are grumpy grandparents when they fry french fries and grease gets on the ground!

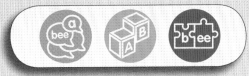

Train Tracks

Identify **tr** and **pr** blends.

truck   tree

present   pretty

train   prince

Have a Slice!

Identify **sl** blend.

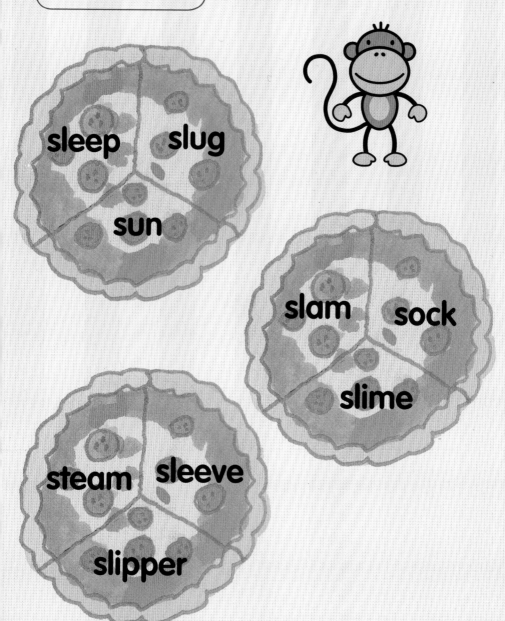

Blend Review

tr

cr

dr

fr

pr

ch

sh

gr

th

br

---

the

ship

green

crack

brown

train

from

drip

chin

pretty

Balloon Blends

Identify **bl**, **cl**, and **fl** blends.

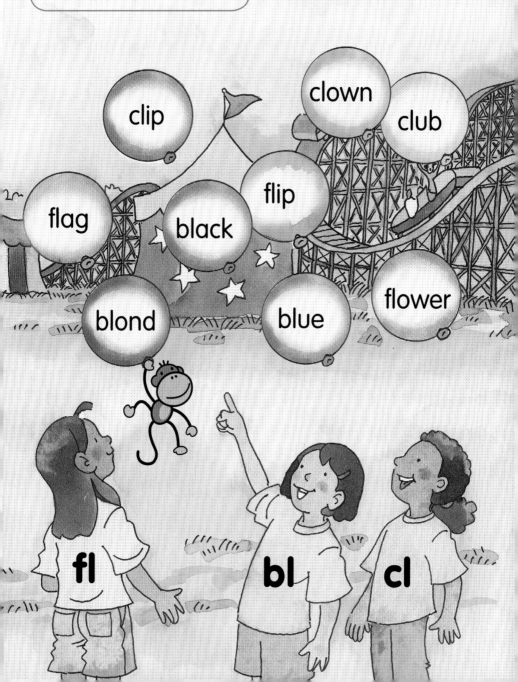

Snap To It!

The letters **s** and **n** blend together
to make the **sn** sound.

snake

sneeze

snore

sneakers

snail

snap

Star Power

The letters **s** and **t** blend together to make the **st** sound.

stamp

pencil

steak

snake

stone

telescope

stool

Be a Spy!

Identify **sp** blend.

The letters **s** and **p** blend together to make the **sp** sound.

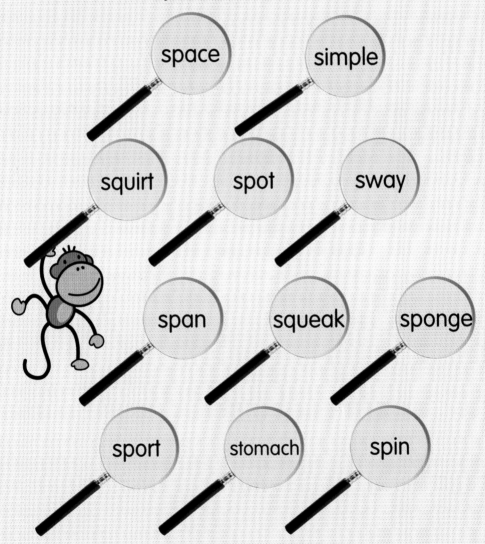

space

simple

squirt

spot

sway

span

squeak

sponge

sport

stomach

spin

Ready, Set, Smile!

The letters **s** and **m** blend together to make the **sm** sound.

smear

mark

snip

mug

small

smack

smash

snow

smell

smooth

smoke

snap

mash

A String of Blends

The letter **r** can be added to **st** or **sp** to make the consonant blends **str** and **spr**.

A kite flies on the end of it. What is it?

You can drink through this. What is it?

You do it when you run fast. What do you do?

It is the season that comes after winter. What is it?

It is what the umpire calls if you swing the bat but miss the ball.

spring   sprint   strike   string   straw

Meet the Knight!

Understand silent **k** in **kn**.

When **kn** starts a word, the **k** is silent. Words that start with **kn** make the **n** sound.

This is the story of one brave knight.

He was known across the land.

He knew how to ride a horse.

He could tie a knot.

He could also knit.

He was quite a knight!

Blend Review

str spr sm st sp
sn bl cl fl

spell snail stick

club strike flip

small spring

black

Oooo La La!

The **oo** sound in **broom** is different from the **oo** sound in **good**.

foot

raccoon

spoon

book

boot

moon

wood

It's a Cow!

When **o** and **w** are joined, they can make the sound heard in **cow**.

cow   cou

brown   broun

cloun   clown

frown   froun

town   toun

croun   crown

R In Charge

The letter **r** changes the sound of some vowels.

play

jar

they

sir

skip

park

star

don't

bird

burn

born

mother

dark

her

car

fur

far

the

bark

cat

Let It Snow!

When **o** and **w** are joined, they can make the long **o** sound heard in **snow**.

crow

brow

row

mow

growl

howl

snow

grow

blow

cow

Our House!

When **o** and **u** are joined, they can make the sound heard in **cloud**.

hound

cost

mouth

ground

moss

count

hint

mouse

Do Your Laundry!

Recognize the **au** sound and spelling pattern.

When **a** and **u** are joined, they can make the sound heard in **laundry**.